Detective Stories

AF196361

Dirty Tricks

Pete and Max
in Action

MIT GEHEIMSCHRIFT FOLIE

Anni Mohn & Julia Gerigk

circon

© Circon Verlag GmbH
Baierbrunner Straße 27, 81379 München
Ausgabe 2022
2. Auflage

Text: Anni Mohn
Illustrationen: Julia Gerigk
Redaktion: Jenny Bux
Übersetzung: Barbara Swayne
Fachredaktion: Stephanie Manz
Produktion: Ute Hausleiter
Titelabbildung: Julia Gerigk
Gestaltung: Roman Bold & Black, Köln
Umschlaggestaltung: Enrico Albisetti

ISBN 978-3-8174-2418-4
381742418/2

Besuchen Sie uns auf Instagram und Facebook: circonverlag

www.circonverlag.de

The first trick

Pete is standing at the big crossroads. He's waiting for his friend Max. He's impatient. Max is late every morning.

'I should tail him one day', Pete thinks. 'Then I can find out why he's never on time. Maybe he sleeps too long.' Pete knows about tailing people. Max and he are famous detectives. Or they'll be famous detectives soon. They haven't got into the newspapers yet. But one day they will.

'Boo!', someone calls from behind. Pete jumps forward and almost ends up on the road.

'You had no idea that I was behind you. Did I frighten you?', Max asks and gives Pete a pat on the back.

trick	Streich
(to) tail	beschatten
on time	pünktlich
(to) frighten	erschrecken
(to) pat on	auf die Schulter
the back	klopfen

3

'Of course, not', Pete answers. 'You can't frighten a detective. Only surprise him.' He gives Max an angry look. 'Now we have to hurry. I hate it when I have to hurry!'
'It keeps us fit', Max says and starts jogging. 'Detectives have to be fit.'
'It's more important to be on time', Pete says. He already finds it difficult to breathe. He's not very sporty.
'You always have to have the last word', Max hisses and runs even faster. This time Pete doesn't answer. Maybe because he's out of breath.

When they come into their classroom, their teacher Ms Potter is surrounded by the other children. 'Who did this?', she asks. 'Who did this?' Her voice is quiet, and she sounds upset. Nobody says a word. 'Look how red he's in the face', Maggie calls out. She points at Pete who is sweating.

out of breath	außer Atem
surrounded	umringt
pile	Haufen
stinking	stinkend
dog-pooh	Hundehaufen
paper plate	Pappteller
(to) glue	kleben
cut-out	ausgeschnitten

'So?', Sophie asks. 'Why do you look like a tomato?
Is there something you want to tell us, Pete?'
'I was only running.' Pete's face becomes even redder.
'What happened?'
'Can't you smell it?', Sophie asks. She asks Maggie
and Jamie to move so that Pete and Max can see
Ms Potter's desk.

On the desk there's a pile of brown, stinking dog-pooh.
The pooh is on a paper plate. Next to it there's a piece
of paper. Someone has glued a message with cut-out
letters from a newspaper: THIS IS WHAT I'M LIKE AS
A TEACHER.

'What do you mean?' Pete is shocked. 'I didn't do that!'
'I believe you', Ms Potter says. 'I can't imagine that you would do something like that.'

'Teacher's pet', Felix whispers.

'Of course, I can't imagine that anybody in my class would do that', Ms Potter says. 'Please go back to your seats now. Pete and Max, could you please take this …' – Ms Potter is looking for the word – 'pile to the large rubbish skip outside? Or to the toilet? Let's start to work now, please.'

Pete waits a little, then he grabs the paper plate with both hands. He holds it as far away from himself as he can and walks through the door that Max has opened for him.

'What a dirty trick', Max says to Pete while they go down the stairs.

'We'll find out who did this', Pete answers. 'Did you see Ms Potter's face?'

teacher's pet	Lehrerliebling
anybody	jemand, irgendjemand
seats	*hier:* Plätze
rubbish skip	Müllcontainer

'Yes.' Max shakes his head. 'I would have been so angry! But Ms Potter looked a little sad. She doesn't get angry, that's her problem.'

'Or it's her good side', Pete answers. 'It's strange, this message with the cut-out letters. Like a letter from a blackmailer. Somebody made a special effort here.'

'Yes, somebody made a very special effort', Max says and points at the paper plate that Pete is carefully carrying down the stairs. But Pete pays no attention to him.

'Maybe Ms Potter was wrong, and it was somebody from our class?', he says.

'Why do you think that?', Max asks.

'Well', Pete says. Now both have stopped. 'Perhaps it has something to do with the offender's handwriting.'

'What?', Max asks. 'I don't understand.'

Can you explain to Max what Pete means?

blackmailer	Erpresser
(to) make a special effort	sich besonders anstrengen
carefully	vorsichtig
offender	Täter

'Ms Potter knows the handwriting of every pupil', Pete says. 'To make sure that she doesn't recognize the handwriting, the person used letters from the newspaper.'

'You're right', Max says.

'Watch out!', Pete suddenly shouts.

'What are you carrying through my school?' Mr Willis, the headmaster, is coming up the stairs.

'This is unbelievable', he says. He raises his finger.
'What's this all about, young man?'
'I was told to take this out', Pete says. 'By Ms Potter.'
'A trick', Max adds.
'Somebody played a trick on Ms Potter? Impossible!
She's one of the best teachers here, don't you think so?'
'That's right', Pete says and nods a few times, which
makes the paper plate move.
'No dancing now', Mr Willis says. 'Take this out
quickly, please.' He runs up the stairs.
'You do it yourself', Pete mumbles and slowly
walks on.

(to) recognize*	wiedererkennen
Watch out!	Achtung!
unbelievable	unerhört, unglaublich
(to) play a trick on	einen Streich spielen
(to) mumble	murmeln

The test

As always during the break Pete and Max sit together on the small wall that surrounds the schoolyard. Max is looking around.
'Look over there, Pete! What's going on?', he asks. Suddenly he's very excited.

Which children are behaving in a strange way?

(to) hang out	herumhängen
matter	Angelegenheit
direction	Richtung
(to) decide	entscheiden

'You mean ██████████████? They have been  hanging out for a few days, whispering to each other', Pete says. 'Do you think they have something to do with the matter?'

'It seems that they have secrets', Max says.

He gives his lunchbox to Pete. 'I'll go over there and pretend that I'm just walking past. Perhaps I can hear what they're talking about.'

'Me too', Pete says. Max shakes his head.

'They'll notice if we both go.
Let me do this alone.'
Pete stays on the wall and
watches Max wander in the
direction of Felix, Sophie and
Matt. But they're careful.
When Max is nearby,
they turn to him and
start talking. They
look angry.

'Should I go and help
him?', Pete thinks for a
moment. Then he decides
to stay where he is. He is
relieved to see that Sophie,
Felix and Matt look more relaxed now.

Once they all look at him. Pete waves, but they keep on talking to each other.
After the break Max goes straight to the school building instead of going back to Pete.
'That's strange', Pete thinks.

When he sits down next to Max in the classroom, his friend pays no attention to him.
'Are you ok?', Pete wants to know, but Max presses his lips together and shakes his head.
Pete is astonished. From the corner of his eye he watches Max. Max takes a piece of paper from his schoolbag and begins to write. He doesn't look at Pete, he doesn't smile. Pete looks at Sophie and Felix who sit in front of him. They turn around and grin.
'Hey', Sophie says to Max, 'are we meeting this afternoon?'
'Sure', Max answers with a smile and lifts a hand.
'Sure', Pete says and also lifts a hand. Max says nothing and looks at the piece of paper.
Sophie and Felix laugh and look at Ms Potter.

(to) wave	winken
straight	geradewegs
astonished	erstaunt
from the corner of the eye	aus dem Augenwinkel
(to) grin	grinsen

'Great. One conversation and Max has new friends', Pete thinks.

'What were you talking about?', Pete asks Max. Max breathes deeply, then turns away from Pete and bends over his piece of paper. His nose almost touches the desk. Pete folds his arms and looks at the blackboard. He doesn't want to show Max how upset he is.

'Please everybody, get a pad and a pencil', Ms Potter says. 'Let's go to the schoolyard. We'll draw a plan of the school.'

Pete is glad that he doesn't have to spend the rest of the school day next to the silent Max. He packs his things and runs out of the classroom.

'Why are you in such a hurry', Felix calls after him. 'Don't you want to wait for your friends?' Then he laughs and adds: 'Oh no, you don't have any friends!'

conversation	Gespräch
(to) bend	sich beugen
pad	Block

Pete looks over at Max. But Max is walking next to Sophie, he's talking to her.

'It doesn't matter', Pete says to himself. 'The best detectives are loners anyway.' He sits on his favourite place on the wall and begins to draw a plan of the school. When he hears a cough, he looks up. It's Max. He walks slowly past Pete but doesn't look at him.

'The guy is totally bonkers', Pete thinks. But suddenly he sees a piece of paper falling from the pocket of Max's trousers. Max stops for a second, looks up at the sky, clears his throat, and walks on.

Pete looks around. Nobody is watching him. He quickly picks up the piece of paper and returns to his wall. When he unfolds the paper, he begins to smile. It's the secret code from the detective book that Max and he have bought together. This code has helped them once before when they had to solve a difficult case.

Can you help Pete with the secret code?

loner	Einzelgänger
anyway	sowieso
cough	Husten
bonkers	bescheuert
(to) clear one's throat	sich räuspern

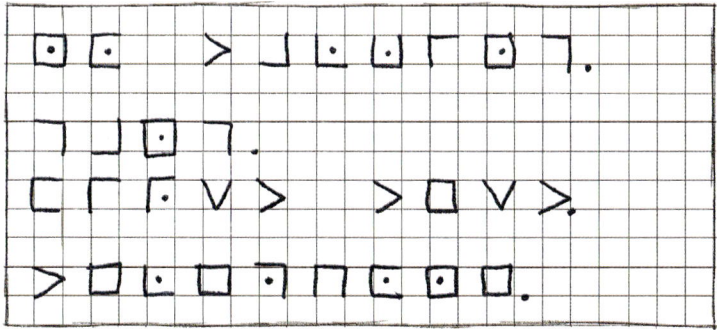

The secret code:

```
A = ⌐   B = ⊔   C = ⌐L   D = ⊐   E = □   F = ⊏
G = ⌐   H = ⊓   I = ⌐    J = ⌐   K = ⊔   L = ⌐L
M = ⊐   N = ⊡   O = ⊏    P = ⌐   Q = ⊓   R = ⌐
S = V   T = >   U = <    V = ∧   W = V   X = >
Y = <   Z = ∧
```

(Freimaurer-Alphabet)

Pete pushes the piece of paper into his trouser pocket.
He takes his pad and walks to the other side of the
school to continue working on his plan. He takes a few
steps backwards to get a better view of the school –
and he almost stumbles over Bonny, the dog. Bonny
belongs to Ms Jenkins, the school secretary.

(to) stumble   stolpern

15

During the lessons Bonny runs around the school grounds. The dog looks at Pete and goes further into the bushes.

'Hey, Bonny, what are you doing there?',
Pete calls out.

And then he sees it. Bonny is doing a pooh.

'Unbelievable!', Pete thinks. He looks at what Bonny has left behind. 'The offender collected what was needed for the trick in the school grounds.'

What does Pete mean?

The dog pooh on the paper plate had the same shape and size as Bonny's.

The Foxes

Today Pete has to walk home alone. After the last lesson Max ran off and left him standing at the school gate. At home Pete has just thrown his schoolbag in the corner when the phone rings.

'Hey Pete', Max says. 'How are you?'

'Can you believe it? The pile on the plate this morning is from Bonny', Pete shouts.

'What's this about?', Max asks.

'The offender has collected dog-pooh from Bonny for the trick', Pete explains impatiently.

'And what can we do with this information?', Max wants to know.

Pete thinks about that. 'Not a lot', he admits. 'Except that the offender probably goes to our school.'

'And now?', Max asks. Pete is silent for a moment.

'Did you find my message?', Max asks.

'Of course', Pete answers. 'I can guess what you wanted to tell me.'

(to) do a pooh	einen Haufen machen
shape*	Form
size*	Größe
(to) admit	zugeben
probably	wahrscheinlich

Can you also guess it?

'I believe that Matt, Sophie and Felix are in a gang', Pete says. 'To become a member of the gang you had to pass an entrance test. You were not allowed to talk to me.'

'Right', Max says. 'Or almost right. I'm never allowed to speak to you again if I want to become a member of the Foxes. That's the name of the gang.'

'Can I also become a member of the Foxes, Max?'

'No', Max says.

'Why?', Pete wants to know.

'They don't want you. I'm sorry.'

'But you want to be with them?', Pete asks. Pete is a little sad that Max never wants to speak to him again in front of other people.

member*	Mitglied
entrance test*	Aufnahmeprüfung
(to) give… a call	… anrufen
spy	Spion
(to) spy on	ausspionieren
fountain	Brunnen
mean	gemein
test of courage	Mutprobe
among	zwischen, inmitten

'Would I give you a call if I really didn't want to speak to you?', Max asks. 'Listen. Have you forgotten that we want to find out whose idea it was to play this dirty trick? I'm a spy now! I spy on the Foxes! If I'm in their gang, I'm sure they'll tell me if they have something to do with the matter.'

'And what's the next thing you have to do to become a member?', Pete asks. 'You wrote: the first test. So there has to be a second test.' Pete is a little jealous of Max. It's really great to be a detective. But to be a spy … that's fantastic!

'This afternoon at four o'clock the Foxes and I will meet at the fountain', Max says. 'Then I'll find out what the next test will be.'

'It seems as if we're on a hot trail', Pete says. 'But it's really mean that we're not allowed to speak to each other. Perhaps the trick on Ms Potter was a test of courage?'

'Yes, maybe. I'll find out! Bye, Pete.' Max has finished the conversation.

'I'll find out?', Pete repeats his last words. 'No, my friend. We'll find out!' He quickly puts on his trainers.

At quarter to four Pete is at the fountain. He doesn't want to be discovered, so he stands among a group of

tour guide — Reiseführer
over there — da drüben

tourists that are looking at the church. The tour guide
points at the church and Pete looks up.
'Do you belong to the group?', an old lady asks him.
'I… no', Pete says. 'My parents are over there.'
He points in the direction of the fountain – and sees
headmaster Willis, Ms Potter and Ms Melon! Ms Melon
is also a teacher at their school. Mr Willis and the
teachers are talking to each other. Maybe they're

talking about the trick this morning? They're coming towards him so Pete hurries away. Then he turns. He's lucky. They haven't noticed him. Now he can follow them. They sit down in the café near the fountain. 'Three coffees, please', Mr Willis says and waves at the waitress.

towards	auf … zu, in Richtung auf
waitress	Kellnerin

'This is perfect', Pete thinks. 'I can listen to what they're saying and keep an eye on the fountain at the same time.'

Pete checks his trouser pocket. Yesterday his mother gave him two Euros. The teachers and the headmaster sit with their backs to the café. So, Pete can go in there and queue up for the ice cream. Now he's very close to their table.

'To be honest', Mr Willis says. 'I'm surprised. And I'm more than pleased.'

'Really?', Ms Melon asks.

'It's wonderful that two excellent teachers who are so popular with everybody apply for this job', Mr Willis says.

'Popular with everybody', Ms Potter repeats. She doesn't sound very happy.

'I always say that teachers who have no problems with their pupils don't have problems with the parents. And parents, well, they're often so difficult nowadays. So … demanding.'

(to) keep an eye on	im Auge behalten
(to) queue up	sich anstellen
popular	beliebt
(to) apply for	sich bewerben
nowadays	heutzutage
demanding	anspruchsvoll

They don't seem to be talking about the trick.

'Now that Ms Peters is headmistress at a new school, I need a new deputy. Not many people want to do that job. That two teachers have applied for it, speaks for our school.' Nobody says anything. Then Mr Willis adds: 'And for me as the boss.'

Pete gets his ice cream.

Mr Willis continues: 'I only wanted to tell you that you're both equally good. I'll need a little more time to decide who will get the job.'

'Of course, Mr Willis', Ms Melon says with a smile and nods a few times. Then she says to Ms Potter: 'I hope you'll manage the problem with your pupils soon, Ms Potter.'

'My problem?', Ms Potter asks and looks astonished. Pete finds this conversation interesting. He forgets to eat his ice cream.

'Well, somebody played a dirty trick on you today. And wasn't there also a letter? What was in the letter?' Ms Melon takes her coffee and slurps it noisily.

headmistress	Direktorin
deputy	Stellvertreter/in
equally	gleichwertig
(to) slurp	schlürfen
noisily	laut, geräuschvoll

'I…', Ms Potter begins to speak, but Mr Willis interrupts her.
'Ms Potter isn't that one of your pupils?', he asks and points towards the fountain. Pete looks as well.
And sees Max. Max is running around the fountain. He's wearing swimming trunks and trainers. He holds a straw hat in his hand and waves it at the people.
'What's the boy doing there?', Ms Potter asks.

Pete has an idea. If that's the second entrance test, it's quite mean – poor Max.

A little girl points at Max and laughs. Pete remembers a nightmare he once had. He was the only person who was dressed up in school. All day long he looked like a pirate while all the others were in their everyday clothes. A terrible nightmare. But he can't help Max now. After all he's not allowed to speak to his friend because of the Foxes.

'What a mess', Pete says to himself quietly. Then he leaves. He decides that Max will never find out that he has seen him in this embarrassing situation.

straw hat	Strohhut
nightmare	Albtraum
dressed up	verkleidet
mess	*hier:* Schweinerei
embarrassing	peinlich

The scarecrow

The next day Pete goes to school early. He doesn't have to wait for Max because Max is not allowed to talk to him.

'We're lucky that Ms Potter is our class teacher', he thinks. After listening to Mr Willis and the teachers yesterday, he doesn't find Ms Melon very nice. When she spoke about the trick, it sounded as if she was even a little pleased that Ms Potter has trouble with her pupils.

When he reaches the school, Maggie waves at him from a distance. 'You have to see this', she calls out. 'Quickly, come into the garden.' Pete starts to run. Some pupils are already in the school garden. They're giggling and whispering to each other.

At first Pete can't see anything special, but then he looks at the scarecrow in the vegetable patch.

Can you see what is special about the scarecrow? Find a picture of the classroom for a clue.

The scarecrow is wearing Mrs Porter's Indeed! The scarecrow is wearing Mrs Porter's yellow raincoat.

On the yellow hat there's a piece of paper with cut-out letters from a newspaper. It says: THIS WORK SUITS ME MUCH BETER.

'Go away, children', Mr Willis shouts. He runs to the scarecrow and pulls at the yellow coat. He's very angry. He takes away the hat and the raincoat and puts them under his arm.

'Tell me immediately who did this!', he shouts at the children. Some of them shake their heads, others simply shrug.

'I'll find out who did this', Mr Willis says. He turns around and walks away. Pete follows him.

'How did the offender get the coat?', he asks the headmaster.

scarecrow	Vogelscheuche
distance	Entfernung
vegetable patch	Gemüsebeet
(to) suit	passen
simply	einfach

'No idea', Mr Willis says. 'Perhaps caretaker Fraser knows more. He unlocks the classrooms every morning.'

'At what time exactly?', Pete asks.

'No idea', Mr Willis replies angrily and walks away. Pete wonders where Mr Fraser could be now. He could be anywhere. It would take too long to look for him. Pete runs upstairs. Ms Jenkins, the school secretary, is always early in her office. Maybe she can help him.

She's actually in her office and Ms Melon and
Mr Fraser are also there. Mr Fraser is bending over
the printer. Pete carefully pulls Mr Fraser's jacket.
'When do you unlock the classroom doors?', he asks.
The caretaker turns around.
'I'm working here, can't you see that?', he grumbles.
'The printer has gone crazy again.'
'It's only a simple question', Pete says.
'At seven', Mr Fraser replies.
'So, after seven o'clock everybody can enter the
classrooms?', Pete asks.
'Yes, sure.' The caretaker stands up and folds his arms.
'If you're thinking about the trick with the raincoat:
Everybody knows that Ms Potter keeps her coat and
her hat in the wardrobe. And if she doesn't lock the
wardrobe, this is her own fault. Why don't you ask her
if the wardrobe was locked? I'm sure that it wasn't.
Ms Potter forgets about these things.'
Ms Melon, who is looking at some papers, laughs out
loud and Mr Fraser smiles at her. Then he says to
Pete: 'I have another question for you: Don't you have
a lesson soon?'

| (to) unlock | aufschließen |

'Mr Fraser is right', Ms Melon says. 'Go to your classroom. I'm sure Ms Potter is sitting there and is very
sad. We're trying to print out a letter to the parents for
her. She's unable to do this at the moment.'
'Do you really believe that Ms Potter gets frightened
that easily?', Pete asks her.
'The lesson begins soon', Ms Melon replies sternly.
Pete turns around to walk away.
'It's time that Ms Potter gets a grip on her pupils',
he hears Ms Melon say. 'They're naughty, all of them.'
'Sometimes I think it would be better if you became
deputy headmistress, Ms Melon', Ms Jenkins says.
'I think Ms Potter can't control her pupils properly.'
Pete runs to his classroom. Ms Potter sits at her desk.
She looks very unhappy. Pete sits down next to Max.
'Do you know about the scarecrow?', he asks him
quietly and Max nods.
After a while Pete adds: 'Did you notice something
in the message?'

unable	nicht imstande
sternly	streng
(to) get a grip on	in den Griff bekommen
properly	ordentlich
(to) spell*	sich schreiben

Max puts his finger in front of his mouth and moves his head in Sophie and Felix's direction.

Did you notice something in the message that was hanging on the scarecrow?

███████████████, Pete writes on a piece of paper and moves it to where Max is sitting.
'Really?', Max writes back.
'███████████████████', Pete whispers.
'Sometimes you really are a teacher's pet', Max whispers back. Felix turns around and looks at them.

Then Felix writes something on a piece of paper and drops it on the floor. He pushes the paper with his left foot to where Max is sitting. Pete looks straight ahead but manages to pick up the paper and give it to Max. The message from Felix says: 'Meeting after school at the field.'

'And I'll be there too', Pete says to himself.

○ Keep out!

When the last lesson is over, Pete is relieved. All day long he has been alone, only Jamie and Maggie have spoken to him during group work in the maths lesson. Even during the break, he had to sit alone on the small wall while Max wandered around the schoolyard with the Foxes.

Slowly Pete packs his things. He wants to give Max and the Foxes a head start. Then he plans to creep up to the playground near the field. He makes his way to the school gate while all the other pupils run past him. He watches Max and the Foxes going towards the field. At the next street corner, he can't see them anymore. When he walks through the school gate, he sees Ms Potter. She's leaning against her car with a piece of paper in her hands. She's shaking her head.

Keep out!	Betreten verboten!
relieved	erleichtert
head start	Vorsprung
(to) creep up	anschleichen
(to) lean against	sich lehnen an

'Have a nice day, Ms Potter', Pete calls. Ms Potter waves at him to come over. She shows him the letter to the parents that she handed out yesterday. She's quite excited.

'On Monday we're going on a trip and look here: meeting at nine o'clock at the train station', she says.

'That's already in my parents' calendar', Pete says. 'Why?'

'But we're meeting at eight o'clock', a very upset Ms Potter says. 'I booked a tour of the museum.'

'Why did you write "at nine o'clock" in the letter if we should meet at eight?', Pete asks.

'If I only knew that', Ms Potter says and looks at the letter again. 'And today is Friday. Now I have to call all the children at home to make sure that they're on time on Monday.'

'You don't have to call me', Pete says. 'I know it now.'

'That helps', Ms Potter says and sighs. 'In the last days everything has gone wrong for me. I'm a little confused.'

(to) hand out	austeilen
trip	Ausflug
train station	Bahnhof
(to) sigh	seufzen
(to) go wrong	schiefgehen
confused	verwirrt

'That's normal', Pete says. 'You want to become deputy headmistress. When my father became boss last year, he behaved really strangely for a few weeks. But that passed.'

'Good to know', Ms Potter says. 'But how do you know that I applied for the job?'

'You can't hide anything from a detective', Pete says proudly.

'I see. But I don't think that I'll become deputy headmistress. The tricks in the last days and now this silly mistake in the letter … Mr Willis must think that I'm unable to do the job.'

'I'll find out who did the tricks', Pete says. Then he takes Ms Potter's hand. 'Goodbye, Ms Potter, I really have to go now.'

Pete runs away to follow the trail of the Foxes.

When he arrives at the field, he can't see anybody. Pete is out of breath. Where could Max be? What test of courage have the Foxes come up with for his friend? Pete looks around. There's a small hill behind the field. He climbs up the hill.

| (to) pass | vorbeigehen |
| (to) come up with… | sich … ausdenken |

At the top he quickly hides behind a big tree trunk. He has discovered the Foxes. Below the hill there's an old farmhouse with a large garden. Felix, Sophie and Matt are leaning against a fence with their backs to Max. They're staring at the apple trees. Now Pete sees Max. He has climbed on a tree and is throwing down apples.

'So, this is the test. They want Max to steal apples. I hope that the owner of the house doesn't catch him.' But everything is very quiet. Nobody seems to be there.

tree trunk	Baumstamm
below	*hier:* unterhalb
(to) catch	*hier:* erwischen
lonely	einsam
ham sandwich	Schinkenbrot
(to) collect	sammeln
(to) appear	erscheinen
(to) bark	bellen

'Lunchtime', Pete thinks. His stomach begins to make noises. During the break he felt so lonely that he couldn't eat his ham sandwich.

'I'll stop this test of courage nonsense now', Pete says to himself.

He walks towards the fence. Max has collected the apples in his t-shirt and is already close to the fence when suddenly a big dog appears. He has come from behind the house and now runs across the field barking loudly. Max turns around.

What a terrible situation: Max is too far away from the apple trees to climb up on one of them. And he's also too far away from the fence. The dog runs so fast, he would catch up with him.

Max starts running in the direction of the fence. 'Stop!', Pete shouts. 'MAX! STOP NOW!' Max freezes and slowly turns around to look at the dog. The apples fall to the ground. The dog is running towards Max and stops just before him. He's growling. His mouth is open, and he shows his teeth. His whole body is tense, at any moment he could jump at Max. 'Max', Pete says quietly. 'Don't move.' Max stands still. Sophie, Matt and Felix are totally quiet. They're as white as sheets.

(to) catch up with	einholen
(to) freeze	*hier:* erstarren
(to) growl	knurren
tense	angespannt
at any moment	jeden Augenblick
sheet	Bettlaken
not at all	gar nicht
(to) face each other	einander gegenüberstehen
backwards	rückwärts
softest voice	sanfteste Stimme

'Don't look into the dog's eyes', Pete says. 'It's best if you don't look at him at all.'

The dog looks at Pete. Then he walks closer to Max, still showing his teeth.

'If he attacks you, you must fall down on the ground, pull up your knees and protect your face', Pete says, again very quietly. Now Max and the dog are facing each other. The dog seems not sure what to do. Pete watches him and thinks that the dog looks a little more relaxed now.

Carefully Pete takes his ham sandwich from his schoolbag. He takes the ham from the bread.

'Look here', Pete says to the dog. He puts his arm through the fence. 'Good ham.'

The dog sniffs and walks a few steps towards him. Pete is so relieved that he almost laughs, but he knows that Max is still in danger. He still has to get across the fence.

'Max', Pete says. 'Try and take a small step backwards. But you mustn't turn around.' Max moves. The dog growls a little louder, but he doesn't follow him. Centimetre by centimetre Max walks backwards to the fence. The dog watches him.

'Come here, sweetie', Pete says in his softest voice, but the dog pays no attention to him.

When Max touches the fence with his back he whispers: 'What now, Pete?'

'Turn around very slowly and come here.'

Max trembles and puts a hand on the fence. When he lifts one foot, the dog moves.

Pete immediately jumps up, stretches out an arm and shouts, 'No! Stop it! Go away!'

Surprised by the very loud voice, the dog turns away. Max gets over the fence.

'Go away!', Pete says to the dog and points at the house. And the dog actually trots away as if nothing had happened.

Max sinks down on his knees and sobs. Sophie, Matt and Felix run to him and hug him.

'Pete has saved my life.' Max gets up again.

Pete suddenly feels tears coming into his eyes and then he becomes very angry.

'What were you idiots thinking? Have you gone crazy?', he shouts at Sophie, Matt and Felix.

'We didn't know that there was a dog in the garden', Sophie says.

'We didn't want this to happen', Felix says. 'Just a little test of courage.'

'So? Are you happy now?' Pete is still very angry.

'What other horrible things were you planning?'

Sophie, Matt and Felix look ashamed.

'And who played the trick on Ms Potter? Was that also a stupid test of courage?'

(to) lift	anheben
(to) trot	traben
(to) sink	sinken
(to) sob	schluchzen
(to) hug	umarmen
horrible	schrecklich, abscheulich
ashamed	beschämt

'We didn't do anything to Ms Potter', Felix says. 'We didn't have to do a test of courage. Only new people that want to be in the Foxes have to pass one.'

'Well, you're real heroes', Pete says. 'Let others suffer while you …'

'Oh, don't get so excited', Sophie says.

'No, now I'm really getting excited', Pete shouts.

Max puts his arm around Pete's shoulders.

'We still have to solve a case. Have you forgotten? These idiots are only holding us up.'

He leads Pete away.

'Why do you know so much about dogs?', Max asks his friend.

'I'm really frightened of big dogs', Pete explains. 'So, I read about dogs. But I would probably have run away screaming and the beast would have torn me to pieces. You were so brave, Max.'

Max smiles. 'I trusted you.'

Pete and Max walk up the hill.

hero	Held
(to) suffer	leiden
(to) hold up	aufhalten
beast	Bestie, Vieh
torn	zerrissen
brave	tapfer, mutig

A battle plan

'That was a total failure', Pete says. He and Max are sitting on the floor in his room. Pete sits in front of his chess board while Max is looking through his football pictures.

'We wasted so much time with this silly gang while the offender is still free out there. Perhaps he's already planning the next trick. What information do we have?' Pete looks for a pencil and a piece of paper. 'The first trick: Ms Potter finds dog-pooh on her desk. Then the scarecrow is dressed up with her clothes. All the things for the tricks have to do with the school: Bonny's pooh and Ms Potter's rain clothes. And then there was the wrong time in the letter to the parents.'

| battle plan | Schlachtplan |
| failure | *hier:* Pleite, Niederlage |

'That wasn't a trick', Max says. 'That was Ms Potter's mistake.'

'Right', Pete admits. Then he remembers something.
'But wait! Perhaps this was a trick too', he says.

'Why do you think that?', Max asks.

'Maybe somebody changed the time at the computer.'

'At the computer?' Max is surprised. 'Which pupil can get to Ms Potter's computer?'

'No pupil', Pete says. 'Three grown-ups are suspects.'

Who is Pete talking about?

'After the trick with the scarecrow I went to the secretary's office. And there I saw our secretary, Ms Jenkins, caretaker Fraser and Ms Melon at the printer. They printed out Ms Potter's letter to the parents. They must have had access to the letter or they couldn't have printed it out. Do you understand?'

Max thinks about this.

'That would be really strange', he says finally. 'Why should they do something like that?'

'Because it seems that one of them doesn't want Ms Potter to become deputy headmistress. I found out that she has applied for the job when I was at the fountain, keeping an eye on you and the Foxes.'

'You were at the fountain?', Max asks. 'Did you see me?'

'No', Pete says quickly.

Max looks at Pete.

'You did see me', he says.

'Only for a moment', Pete admits. And he begins to laugh although he doesn't want to. 'You were looking so …'

'Shut up!' Max grabs a pawn and throws it at Pete. Then he jumps up. 'So now we investigate the grown-ups! Pete, we're becoming better and better.'

'You're right', Pete says. 'But grown-ups are tough opponents. Sometimes they can be very clever.'

'It's not so difficult. We only have to keep an eye on one person. The one who really doesn't want Ms Potter to become deputy headmistress', Max says.

'You mean Ms Melon?', Pete asks.

Max nods.

'But what about the mistake in the letter that was attached to the scarecrow? Ms Melon would never make such a bad spelling mistake. She's a teacher', Pete says.

grown-up	Erwachsene/r
access	Zugang
although	obwohl
pawn	Bauer (Schachfigur)
tough	*hier:* hart
opponent	Gegner

'Or she's clever. She made the mistake on purpose',
Max replies.

'That's what I mean: grown-ups …' Pete sighs.

'Ms Jenkins wouldn't like it if Ms Potter becomes
deputy headmistress and caretaker Fraser seemed to
agree with her.'

'Perhaps we should look for a grown-up in school who
can help us. A grown-up who knows all the suspects',
Max suggests.

'You mean …' Pete smiles.

Which person are the boys thinking about?

'Exactly! Headmaster Willis', Max says.

'Pete, we need your parent's computer.
We'll look for his address on the
internet. I know
how to do that. We
must talk to him.'

A little later they stand in front of the headmaster's house.

'You ring the doorbell', Max says.

'No, you do it', Pete says.

'It doesn't really matter', Max thinks and rings the bell. 'He can't see which one of us has rung the bell when he opens the door.'

'And you talk to him', Pete says.

'No, you do.'

'You're the brave guy who stands up to wild dogs', Pete says.

'And you're the clever guy who plays chess', Max replies.

on purpose	mit Absicht
(to) seem to agree	einverstanden zu sein scheinen
(to) stand up to	sich entgegenstellen

At that moment headmaster Willis opens the door.

'What do you want?', he asks.

Pete and Max look at each other and say nothing.

'So?', Mr Willis asks a little impatiently.

'We have to talk to you', Pete says.

'It's urgent', Max says.

'I just wanted to have a coffee and a piece of cake. It's Sunday!', Mr Willis says. 'Headmasters also need their weekend.'

'A piece of cake would be great', Pete says and steps into the house.

'Okay', Mr Willis sighs. 'Come in.'

After the boys have told him what they know, Mr Willis nods.

'To be honest, I was also a little suspicious. Or do you believe that I wasn't wondering what's going on?'

'Why should we believe that?', Max asks.

Mr Willis drinks some coffee. 'It doesn't matter. After you spoke to me in the schoolyard, Pete, I began to think. Sometimes headmasters also think about things. The school rooms are unlocked at seven o'clock in the morning and the school gate opens at quarter to eight. At that time the scarecrow was already dressed up.'

'That confirms our suspicion', Pete says.

Why does Pete say that this confirms their suspicion?

'This means, the offender must have a key to the school . Somebody needed a key to get into the classroom and fetch Ms Potter's coat and hat before the school gate was unlocked', Pete says.

'And who has a key to the school?', Max wants to know.

'All the teachers, Ms Jenkins and caretaker Fraser', Mr Willis says. He gets up from his chair and walks around. 'Oh, this is so unpleasant. On Wednesday the mayor comes because of the gym. The press will be there. What if something happens? That would be so embarrassing! We really need a new gym. Mr Fraser has made a list of all the broken things in the gym. I want to show it to the mayor. If somebody plays a dirty trick, that would be a disaster! Who wants to give money to a school in chaos?'

Pete takes a piece of cake. Suddenly he has an idea. 'And what if we catch the offender before Wednesday? I have a plan …'

urgent	dringend
suspicious	*hier:* misstrauisch
(to) confirm	bestätigen
suspicion	Verdacht
unpleasant	unerfreulich
mayor	Bürgermeister
press	Presse
broken	kaputt
disaster	Katastrophe

A trap

On Tuesday, the day after the school trip, Max and Pete are in school on time. Mr Willis is already waiting for them.
'There you are', he says and quickly walks up the stairs. 'Come with me!'

In front of his office he looks left and right. 'The coast is clear', he whispers, and the boys follow him into his office. He shuts the door and sits down at his desk. He folds his arms behind his head and smiles at the boys. 'While you had a nice day with Ms Potter yesterday, I did my homework', he says proudly.

'That's great', Pete says.

'I spoke to Ms Jenkins, Mr Fraser and Ms Melon and told them that an embarrassing situation like the one with the scarecrow mustn't happen again. Under no circumstances! I asked them to keep their eyes open and inform me immediately about anything suspicious.'

'Very good', Max says. 'And what did they say?'

'They all said that they would help me', he answers. 'And they will. I'm the headmaster after all.'

'Sure!' Pete nods. 'And did you also complain about the naughty children?'

'Of course, I did. That was very easy for me'.

trap	Falle
the coast is clear	die Luft ist rein
under no circumstances	unter keinen Umständen

He grins at Max and Pete. 'That was a joke. Even headmasters make jokes sometimes.'

'Only very good headmasters', Pete adds to please Mr Willis.

'Do you think the plan will work?', Max asks. 'Do you think that there will be another trick today or tomorrow?'

'Yes, I do! Because I also said that Ms Potter will not become deputy headmistress if something happens again.'

What do you think the plan is?

'Brilliant', Pete says. 'Very good, Mr Willis! We have set a super trap for the three suspects.  Now it seems as if the mayor's visit is the best opportunity* to harm* Ms Potter. The offender only has to think about a trick that makes Ms Potter look really bad.'

joke	Scherz
(to) please	eine Freude machen
opportunity*	Gelegenheit
(to) harm*	*hier:* schaden

'We have to catch the person red-handed otherwise we have no proof', Max says.

'I'm sure that we'll manage that', Mr Willis says.

'During the day there's too much going on here in school. All the tricks were prepared during the night or early in the morning. Tonight I'll stay in school and keep watch.'

'Too bad that we can't be there', Pete says sadly.

'Children belong in their beds at night, we spoke about that already.' Mr Willis goes to the window. 'I'll be everywhere and keep an eye on everything. You don't have to worry.'

Max and Pete look at each other.

'We trust you completely', Pete says.

'Good luck!', Max says.

Headmaster Willis raises a thumb.

red-handed	auf frischer Tat
proof	Beweis
(to) keep watch*	Wache halten
(to) raise a thumb	Daumen in die Höhe strecken

Surprise in the morning

The two master detectives can't be stopped by anybody, not even a headmaster. Children have to be in their beds at night, that's right. But detectives have to be in the place that could become a crime scene, that's clear! If you're a detective and a child, you have to decide what is more important.

When the alarm clock rings, Pete rubs his eyes. It's half past four in the morning. He hopes that Max and he are right about the time. They think something will happen when the sun rises. Why should somebody walk around the school ground in the dark with a torch? People would notice that.

Pete jumps out of bed. He writes a note and puts it on his pillow: 'Already at school – important! Don't worry.' Who knows if he'll be back home when his mother comes to wake him up.

Quietly he makes his way down the stairs and opens the front door. He stops for a moment and listens. Nothing. He shuts the door carefully and runs off.

'I hope that I don't have to wait for Max again', he thinks.

But Max is already at the big crossroads.

'Let's go', he whispers.

It's strange to be out on the street so early in the morning. All the windows are dark, and the pavements are empty. There are no cars. It gives Pete goose pimples.

'You're quite fast', Max says. 'Are you frightened?' 'Not at all', Pete says. 'I want to get to the school before something happens.' Max and Pete are running faster and faster. When they reach the school gate, they're both out of breath. They climb across the gate.

crime scene	Tatort
alarm clock	Wecker
(to) rise	*hier:* aufgehen
torch	Taschenlampe
front door	Haustür
pavement	Gehweg
goose pimples	Gänsehaut

'Okay', Pete says. 'Let's have a look around.'
They run to the school garden. It starts to get light.
It's totally quiet.
'It looks the same as every day here', Pete says.
They walk along the school to the gym. They can't see
anything unusual there. They walk around a corner
and stop under the window of the headmaster's office.
'Do you hear that?', Max asks. Snoring.
'Mr Willis is asleep!' Pete is upset. 'He said he would
keep watch!'
Max picks up a small stone and throws it against
the window. He listens.

'He's still snoring', Max says
and picks up another stone.
'How can one sleep so deeply
and snore so loudly?', Pete
asks. He also picks up
a stone.

But Mr Willis doesn't wake up, not even after they
have thrown twenty stones at the window.
'It doesn't matter. We'll do the next round alone',
Max says.
They start again at the school gate, then they walk
through the garden at the back of the school and then
they reach the gym again.
'That's impossible! That's …' On the gym wall it says
in capital letters:
THE GYM MUST GO AND MS POTER TOO!

'This wasn't there earlier. Somebody painted it while
we were trying to wake up Mr Willis', Max says.
'Unbelievable!', Pete shouts.

snoring	Schnarchen
capital letter	Großbuchstabe

'What are you doing here?', calls a loud voice behind them. A heavy hand lands on Pete's shoulder. Pete and Max scream.

'You should be in bed and sleep!', Mr Willis is angry. 'And who painted this on the wall?'

'We would like to know that too', Pete says and puts a hand on his heart.

'I've just walked around the school grounds. This must have happened then.'

Pete and Max look at him. They know exactly what he had just done.

'A headmaster can't be everywhere at the same time', Mr Willis defends himself.

'And now?', Pete asks. 'We still don't know who did this!'

'But we noticed it early enough', Mr Willis says. 'You two go home now and I'll fetch some paint and a brush from the cellar. I'll sort this out, no problem.' He points a finger first at Pete and then at Max. 'You go back to bed immediately. We'll meet again when school starts.'

(to) defend	verteidigen
paint	Farbe
brush	Pinsel
(to) sort out	in Ordnung bringen

The evidence

Pete is so angry at Mr Willis that he can't go to sleep.
It was his job to keep watch in the school. But he slept!
And because he and Pete tried to wake him up, they
didn't notice who wrote the message on the gym wall.
'Grown-ups are good for nothing', Pete mumbles when
he gets out of bed the second time this morning.
'They just don't take things seriously.'

Max is also in a bad mood when they meet at the
crossroads. 'Our plan was good, but when you have
only lousy staff what can you do?', he says.
'Absolutely', Pete agrees. 'If we hadn't tried to wake
up Mr Willis, we would have noticed what happened.'
When they arrive at the school, they run to the gym
immediately. Did the headmaster remove the paint?
Otherwise Ms Potter will be terribly upset.

evidence	Beweis
(to) go to sleep	einschlafen
seriously	ernst
bad mood	schlechte Laune
lousy	lausig
staff	Mitarbeiter

Mr Willis is standing in front of the gym. He's covered in blue paint. 'Fortunately, I could remove this embarrassment from the wall', he says.

'You did an excellent job, Mr Willis', Ms Melon replies and the headmaster nods. All the teachers are standing in front of the wall. Pete goes to Ms Potter and shakes her hand.

'It's all right', she says quietly and holds his hand for a moment. 'But I don't understand why somebody hates me so much.'

'I don't believe that somebody hates you', Pete says. 'This person doesn't want you to become deputy headmistress.'

He looks at the people around him very seriously.

'Isn't that so, Mr Fraser?'

'What do you mean?', the caretaker asks him.

Do you have an idea, what Pete could have discovered?

‘There's green paint on your jacket’, Pete says. ‘Exactly like the paint that was on the wall. We saw what was written there before Mr Willis painted over it.’
Caretaker Fraser goes very red in the face.
‘What a cheek!’, he screams. ‘The stain … that's been on my jacket for weeks.’ He turns around to Mr Willis. ‘You see how dirty the jacket is? There are stains everywhere. And how does the boy know that it's the same paint as on the wall? You can't see anything now!’ He points at the fresh blue paint.
Pete thinks for a moment. Then he says: ‘Mr Willis, you told me that Mr Fraser gave you a list of all the broken things in the gym. Could I please see this list?’
Headmaster Willis rummages through his pocket.
‘It must be somewhere …’, he mumbles, ‘… here it is. But why do you want it, Pete?’
‘I just want to read it’, Pete says and takes the piece of paper.

fortunately	glücklicherweise
embarrassment	Peinlichkeit
What a cheek!	Was für eine Frechheit!

What do you think Pete hopes to find in the list?

He calls out after a while: 'There it is! ███████ ████ ████ ██ ████ ██████ ████ ████ ███ ██ You didn't pay much attention at school, did you, ███████ ?'
The caretaker breathes in deeply.
'I…' he begins. But at this moment Ms Melon puts a hand on his arm.
'Why did you do that?', she asks in a very soft voice.
'Because … because I love you.' Mr Fraser has tears in his eyes. 'And you really wanted to become deputy headmistress. So, I thought I could help a little bit.'

'That's the most romantic thing anybody has ever done for me', Ms Melon says. She kisses Mr Fraser on the cheek.

'I have actually applied for a job at another school. Yesterday I had the letter that said they have accepted me. I thought that private life and working life should be separate! At the beginning of the next school year I'll start at the school at the pond as deputy headmistress.'

'If that's the case, I appoint you as deputy headmistress at our school, Ms Potter', Mr Willis says. 'The first thing we have to do together is to dismiss Mr Fraser.'

Mr Fraser stares at the floor. 'Yes, you should do that, Ms Potter. I've deserved it. I'm really sorry.'

Ms Potter looks at Ms Melon and then at caretaker Fraser.

'You're the best caretaker in the world', she says after a while. 'Why should we dismiss you? You went a little crazy because you're in love. What do you think, Mr Willis?'

Mr Willis thinks about this for a moment. Then he nods and smiles.

cheek	Wange
(to) accept	annehmen
private life	Privatleben
working life	Berufsleben
pond	Teich, Weiher
(to) appoint	ernennen
(to) dismiss	entlassen

'Then we simply forget about the whole thing',
Ms Potter says, looking very pleased.
'Great. If Mr Fraser doesn't go to prison, we don't
get into the papers again', Max whispers to Pete.
'Don't be so heartless', Pete says.

But the next day there's a photo of Pete, Max and
the mayor on page ten of the newspaper. The headline
says: Pupils are happy! And underneath: Mayor
supports new gym building!
'You see', Pete says. 'Now all the readers at least
know our faces, even if they don't know yet that
we're detectives.'

prison	Gefängnis
heartless	herzlos
(to) support	unterstützen

Wörterverzeichnis

(to) accept	annehmen
access	Zugang
(to) admit	zugeben
alarm clock	Wecker
although	obwohl
among	zwischen, inmitten
anybody	jemand, irgendjemand
anyway	sowieso
(to) appear	erscheinen
(to) apply for	sich bewerben
(to) appoint	ernennen
ashamed	beschämt
astonished	erstaunt
at any moment	jeden Augenblick
backwards	rückwärts
bad mood	schlechte Laune
(to) bark	bellen
battle plan	Schlachtplan
beast	Bestie, Vieh
below	*hier:* unterhalb
(to) bend	sich beugen
blackmailer	Erpresser
bonkers	bescheuert
brave	tapfer, mutig

broken	kaputt
brush	Pinsel
capital letter	Großbuchstabe
carefully	vorsichtig
(to) catch	*hier:* erwischen
(to) catch up with	einholen
cheek	Wange
(to) clear one's throat	sich räuspern
(to) collect	sammeln
(to) come up with…	sich … ausdenken
(to) confirm	bestätigen
confused	verwirrt
conversation	Gespräch
cough	Husten
(to) creep up	anschleichen
crime scene	Tatort
cut-out	ausgeschnitten
(to) decide	entscheiden
(to) defend	verteidigen
demanding	anspruchsvoll
deputy	Stellvertreter/in
direction	Richtung
disaster	Katastrophe
(to) dismiss	entlassen
distance	Entfernung
(to) do a pooh	einen Haufen machen

dog-pooh	Hundehaufen
dressed up	verkleidet
embarrassing	peinlich
embarrassment	Peinlichkeit
entrance test	Aufnahmeprüfung
equally	gleichwertig
evidence	Beweis
(to) face each other	einander gegenüber- stehen
failure	*hier:* Pleite, Niederlage
fortunately	glücklicherweise
fountain	Brunnen
(to) freeze	*hier:* erstarren
(to) frighten	erschrecken
from the corner of the eye	aus dem Augenwinkel
front door	Haustür
(to) get a grip on	in den Griff bekommen
(to) give… a call	… anrufen
(to) glue	kleben
goose pimples	Gänsehaut
(to) go to sleep	einschlafen
(to) go wrong	schiefgehen
(to) grin	grinsen
(to) growl	knurren
grown-up	Erwachsene/r

ham sandwich	Schinkenbrot
(to) hand out	austeilen
(to) hang out	herumhängen
(to) harm	*hier:* schaden
head start	Vorsprung
headmistress	Direktorin
heartless	herzlos
hero	Held
(to) hold up	aufhalten
horrible	schrecklich, abscheulich
(to) hug	umarmen
joke	Scherz
(to) keep an eye on	im Auge behalten
Keep out!	Betreten verboten!
(to) keep watch	Wache halten
(to) lean against	sich lehnen an
(to) lift	anheben
lonely	einsam
loner	Einzelgänger
lousy	lausig
(to) make a special effort	sich besonders anstrengen
matter	Angelegenheit
mayor	Bürgermeister
mean	gemein
member	Mitglied

mess	*hier:* Schweinerei
(to) mumble	murmeln
nightmare	Albtraum
noisily	laut, geräuschvoll
not at all	gar nicht
nowadays	heutzutage
offender	Täter
on purpose	mit Absicht
on time	pünktlich
opponent	Gegner
opportunity	Gelegenheit
out of breath	außer Atem
over there	da drüben
pad	Block
paint	Farbe
paper plate	Pappteller
(to) pass	vorbeigehen
(to) pat on the back	auf die Schulter klopfen
pavement	Gehweg
pawn	Bauer (Schachfigur)
pile	Haufen
(to) play a trick on	einen Streich spielen
(to) please	eine Freude machen
pond	Teich, Weiher
popular	beliebt
press	Presse
prison	Gefängnis

private life	Privatleben
probably	wahrscheinlich
proof	Beweis
properly	ordentlich
(to) queue up	sich anstellen
(to) raise a thumb	Daumen in die Höhe strecken
(to) recognize	wiedererkennen
red-handed	auf frischer Tat
relieved	erleichtert
(to) rise	*hier:* aufgehen
rubbish skip	Müllcontainer
scarecrow	Vogelscheuche
seats	*hier:* Plätze
(to) seem to agree	einverstanden zu sein scheinen
seriously	ernst
shape	Form
sheet	Bettlaken
(to) sigh	seufzen
simply	einfach
(to) sink	sinken
size	Größe
(to) slurp	schlürfen
snoring	schnarchen
(to) sob	schluchzen

softest voice	sanfteste Stimme
(to) sort out	in Ordnung bringen
(to) spell	sich schreiben
spy	Spion
(to) spy on	ausspionieren
staff	Mitarbeiter
(to) stand up to	sich entgegenstellen
sternly	streng
stinking	stinkend
straight	geradewegs
straw hat	Strohhut
(to) stumble	stolpern
(to) suffer	leiden
(to) suit	passen
(to) support	unterstützen
surrounded	umringt
suspicion	Verdacht
suspicious	*hier:* misstrauisch
(to) tail	beschatten
teacher's pet	Lehrerliebling
tense	angespannt
test of courage	Mutprobe
the coast is clear	die Luft ist rein
torch	Taschenlampe
torn	zerrissen
tough	*hier:* hart
tour guide	Reiseführer
towards	auf … zu, in Richtung auf

train station	Bahnhof
trap	Falle
tree trunk	Baumstamm
trick	Streich
trip	Ausflug
(to) trot	traben
unable	nicht imstande
unbelievable	unerhört, unglaublich
under no circumstances	unter keinen Umständen
(to) unlock	aufschließen
unpleasant	unerfreulich
urgent	dringend
vegetable patch	Gemüsebeet
waitress	Kellnerin
Watch out!	Achtung!
(to) wave	winken
What a cheek!	Was für eine Frechheit!
working life	Berufsleben